2/13

BIG SWAMP BEASTS

Michael Cox

ILLUSTRATIONS BY CHUCK WHELON

BLOOMSBURY

LONDON   NEW DELHI   NEW YORK   SYDNEY

Published 2013 by
Bloomsbury Publishing Plc
50 Bedford Square, London, WC1B 3DP

www.bloomsbury.com
www.storiesfromthezoo.com

ISBN 978-1-4088-3576-0

Picture acknowledgements:
Cover images: Shutterstock.
Inside images all Shutterstock apart from the following:p14 Roman coin inset ©http://www.beastcoins.com/RomanImperial/IV-III/OtaciliaSevera/Z5253.jpg, p15 top inset ©F. York/ZSL, p19 top inset ©ZSL, p20 top inset ©ZSL, p28 square inset ©Greg Greer Enterprises Inc., p42 top inset ©SuperStock, p50 top inset ©Will Merydith via Flickr Creative Commons, p88 inset ©SuperStock, p74 top inset ©Steven G. Johnson via Flickr Creative Commons, p72 inset ©Elizabeth Kendall via Flickr Creative Commons, p73 inset ©Joachim S. Mueller via Flickr Creative Commons, p74 bottom inset ©Ravas51 via Flickr Creative Commons, p76 inset ©Brian Gatwicke via Flickr Creative Commons, p79 ©Brian Gatwicke via Flickr Creative Commons, p82 inset ©Sergey Pisarevskiy via Flickr Creative Commons, p84 bottom inset ©Ted via Flickr Creative Commons, p86 inset ©Andreas Schluter via Flickr Creative Commons, p87 inset ©Hugo Claessen via Flickr Creative Commons, p89 inset ©SuperStock, p90 background ©SuperStock.

Manufactured and supplied under licence from the Zoological Society of London.

Produced for Bloomsbury Publishing Plc by Gridlock Design
www.gridlock-design.co.uk

A CIP catalogue for this book is available from the British Library.

Printed in China by C&C Offset Printing Co., Ltd.

1 3 5 7 9 10 8 6 4 2

3/0172 438 43

Michael Cox

BIG SWAMP BEASTS

Monstrously muddy swamp beast facts!

CONTENTS

INTRODUCTION

SWAMP BEASTS!

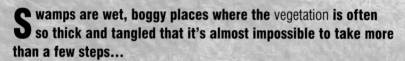

Swamps are wet, boggy places where the vegetation is often so thick and tangled that it's almost impossible to take more than a few steps...

They're scary, mysterious and treacherous places, too, where one wrong move can lead to a careless explorer being sucked down until they're neck deep in stinking goo. Swamps come alive at night, the air filled with strange hooting, clicking and hissing noises, occasionally interrupted by blood-curdling roars and chilling screams.

Wading in all that stinking ooze are humongous great beasts, which would think nothing of biting a human in two. Swimming just below the surface of the murky water are lethal, **sinuous** creatures capable of electrocuting an unwary adventurer from metres away.

Concealed in the undergrowth are massive coiled serpents, which could crush and swallow a small child in one go. Or lying so perfectly still that they appear to be nothing more dangerous than rotting logs, are enormous, scaly, prehistoric killing-machines!

Welcome, do come in!

A hidden bullfrog. Well, almost!

And finally… hidden in the mud are bizarre fish which can walk on land and climb trees, enormous lizards that dig up and eat dead bodies, beasts with horns the size of a grown man, and totally weird amphibians whose babies hatch straight out of their skin!

Swamps are awesome. And the beasts, which live in them are even more awesome. So what are you waiting for? Come on in!

1 THE HIPPOPOTAMUS

AFRICA'S MOST NOTORIOUS SERIAL KILLER

The awesome creatures we call hippopotamuses have been around for about 20 million years. There were even hippos wandering around Britain 125,000 years ago and their remains have been discovered under Trafalgar Square in London.

After the elephant and white rhino, the hippo is the largest land animal on Earth. Hippos have to stay in water for most of the day so they can keep cool in the baking heat of the African sun. They can't swim but they are able to glide quite gracefully along swamp, lake and river beds. However they have to rise to the surface every five minutes or so to take air into their massive lungs.

Habitat loss is a big problem

HIPPOS IN DANGER

Don't be fooled by hippos' slightly cuddly and 'bumbling' appearance. They are incredibly aggressive creatures and kill more humans in Africa than any other land animal. They're fiercely possessive of their **territory** and anyone setting foot on their 'turf' risks suffering a very ghastly death. In one very gruesome attack in Tanzania, a hippo overturned a tourist's canoe, then, with one single crunch of its huge, razor sharp tusks, it bit off his head and shoulders! You have been warned.

Common hippos are classed as a **vulnerable species**, and there are only about 125,000 of them left in the wild. The biggest threat to hippos is habitat loss, but they are also killed for meat, for their teeth (which are used as a kind of ivory), and by big game hunters for so-called 'sport'!

THE CUTAWAY HIPPO

Eyes: Situated on top of the head so the hippo can submerge most of its body in water whilst still being able to see, the eyes are covered by a clear membrane (almost like goggles) for protection underwater.

Head: Massive with a wide snout, large nostrils and very small ears. A hippo can close both its nostrils and its ears underwater.

Teeth: Razor sharp incisors and two pairs of tusk-like **canine** teeth of up to 50 centimetres (20 inches) long make the hippo a formidable killer.

Mouth: Enormous, with lips up to 70 centimetres (almost 30 inches) wide. A hippo can open its mouth over one metre (three feet) wide, that's big enough to bite a small boat in half.

Throat: A large **larynx** (voice box) creates low frequency sounds, which can be heard for miles underwater.

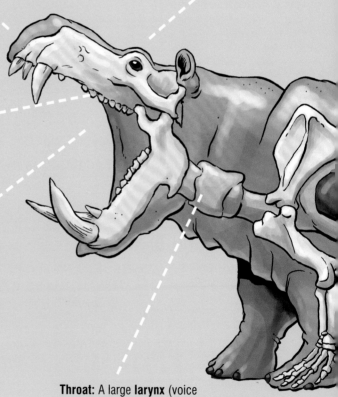

Body size: Can grow up to five metres (17 feet) long and can weigh in excess of 3,000 kilograms (6,600 pounds).

Height: Shoulder height of one and a half metres (five feet).

Stomach: Three metres (ten feet) long, the stomach is **multi-chambered** to slow down and improve digestion.

Body: Barrel-shaped torso to aid flotation.

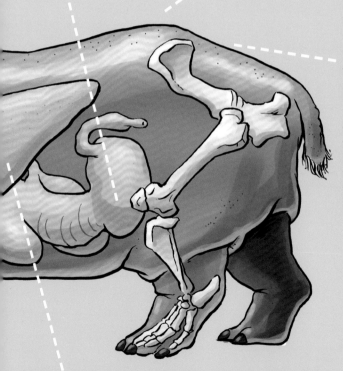

Skin: Varies from brown to greyish purple with pink underparts. A hippo's skin is usually about 15 centimetres (six inches) thick and can weigh up to 500 kilograms (1,100 pounds). It has lots of folds and creases, and is hairless (a hippo only has bristles on its nose, ears and tail).

Lungs: Large lungs fill the hippo's torso and take in air quickly so the hippo can stay submerged for long periods of time. A hippo must return to the surface of the water to breathe every four to six minutes. A sleeping hippo can surface to breathe and return to the riverbed without waking up.

ONE BIG HAPPY FAMILY... WELL, ALMOST!

Hippos live in groups of about 30 to 100 animals known as pods, bloats or sieges. Each pod contains cow hippos (ladies) and young bulls (gents), and is ruled over by one mega-bossy bull hippo.

The boss bull can **mate** with all the females and also occasionally allows the young bulls to mate with the females. When rival bulls meet they stand nose to nose with their mouths open as wide as they'll go. If they decide to fight, they slash at each other with their massive tusks, bellowing savagely whilst swinging their enormous heads like sledgehammers. Most bull hippos have got lots of battle scars and some are even killed in fights.

HIPPO 'HAPPY EVENTS'

Hippos mate in the water (not wishing to embarrass passing giraffes and baboons). Sometimes the females are completely submerged during mating and have to keep sticking their head above the surface to take in air. Eight months later they give birth to a bouncing baby hippo, which weighs about 42 kilograms (93 pounds). When they're little, young hippos stand on their mums' backs so that they don't drown in deep water.

THE HIPPO INSECT REMOVER

In cartoons and comic books, you'll often see a hippo and a small bird spending time together, as if they're best mates. And that really does happen. The bird is called an oxpecker, and it sits on the skin of hippos and other big animals and eats up all the lice, fleas and other creepy-crawly things that like to live there. The hippo gets a hoover, while the oxpecker gets an easy meal.

Two males fight

Oxpeckers love to hoover hippos

NINE AWESOME HIPPO FACTS!

1 Hippos need to fill their massive lungs with air before they dive underwater. To prevent their lungs acting as flotation chambers and sending them straight back to the surface, the bones in their legs are completely solid with no **marrow** and act just like the belted weights that divers use.

3 There are wild hippos in South America – but only a few. A Columbian gangster kept four pet ones in his private zoo. Eventually, they were left to roam wild in the surrounding jungle and bred, killing cows and attacking humans.

4 In AD 248, the Roman emperor Philip I brought hippos to ancient Rome to fight gladiators in the arena. He also had silver coins **minted** with a picture of a hippo on them.

2 The Greek name, hippopotamus means 'river horse'. Until 1909 naturalists thought hippos were related to pigs. But we now know the hippo's closest animal relative is the whale. They share similar **DNA** and it's thought that they started setting out on their separate **evolutionary routes** about 55 million years ago.

5 The first hippo to be exhibited in a zoo in modern times was called Obaysch. He came to ZSL London Zoo from Egypt in 1850. Thousands of people flocked to see him every day, even though he was famous for his grumpiness. He was so popular that someone wrote a song about him called the 'Hippopotamus Polka'.

6 Hippos communicate by grunting, braying, bellowing, and clicking. A bull hippo's bellow measures an ear-shattering 115 decibels, which is as loud as the roar of the mighty lion.

7 Despite the fact that a mum hippo is pregnant for eight months, which is just one month short of the time for a human pregnancy, when their young are born, they're ten times the size of human babies.

8 Hippos only leave the water to feed at night. They find their way to their feeding grounds by following the trail of hippo poo they've splattered out on previous nights.

9 Sometimes hippo pods can contain up to 1,000 animals, especially in the dry season when bathing pools are scarce.

FACTOR 15... FOR HIPPOS

Hippos' hides have lots of little glands which squirt out thick, oily, red liquid, which is often referred to as 'blood sweat'. But really, it's neither blood nor sweat. In fact, the liquid is a kind of skin protection for the hippos.

The 'blood sweat', as it's commonly referred to, contains a sort of sun-screen lotion which stops the hippo's exposed skin cracking and burning in the hot sun. It also contains antiseptic which, despite the fact that hippos wallow in water filled with their own poo, ensures that their wounds heal quickly without becoming infected.

HIPPO SAFETY TIPS

1 When a hippo yawns at you it's not a sign of tiredness or boredom, it's telling you it doesn't like you and might well attack you.

2 Hippos can run faster than humans, often reaching speeds of 30 kilometres (18 miles) per hour. They can also climb steep banks.

3 If a hippo does decide to attack, it will charge at you bellowing ferociously, with its mouth wide open and its massive teeth bared in readiness to bite you.

4 Never get between a hippo and water, or a hippo and its **calf**. It will attack you!

5 If a hippo looks like it's about to attack, the best line of defence is to climb the nearest tree and wait for the hippo to get bored and go away.

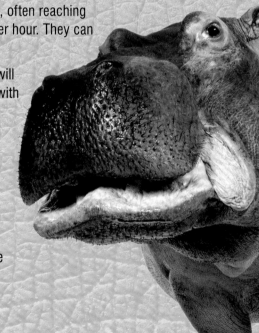

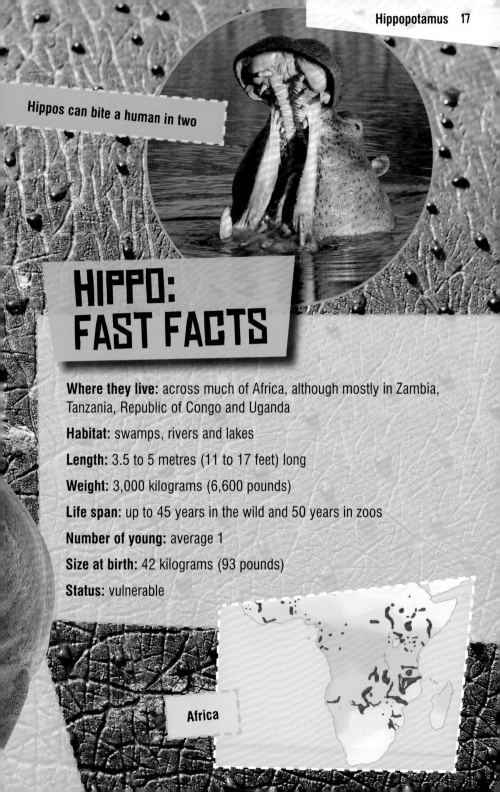

Hippos can bite a human in two

HIPPO:
FAST FACTS

Where they live: across much of Africa, although mostly in Zambia, Tanzania, Republic of Congo and Uganda

Habitat: swamps, rivers and lakes

Length: 3.5 to 5 metres (11 to 17 feet) long

Weight: 3,000 kilograms (6,600 pounds)

Life span: up to 45 years in the wild and 50 years in zoos

Number of young: average 1

Size at birth: 42 kilograms (93 pounds)

Status: vulnerable

Africa

2 THE PYGMY HIPPOPOTAMUS

SMALL... AND VERY, VERY SHY

Pygmy hippos look like smaller versions of common full-size hippos. And they're similar to them in several ways: they sweat the same 'factor 15' skin protection as the big ones do, 'yawn' as a threat display, must remain near water all the time, are herbivores and emerge from the water at night in order to feed.

1 They're only half as tall as their massive common hippo cousins and are less than a quarter of their weight.

2 They're not nearly as stroppy as common hippos. Rather than squaring up for a fight, if they feel threatened, pygmy hippos are far more likely to trot off into the undergrowth and hide until the danger has passed. Nevertheless, you still wouldn't want to tangle with a pygmy hippo.

3 Rather than living in large groups, like common hippos do, pygmy hippos live alone or in a small family consisting of mum, dad and their calf, or just mum and her calf.

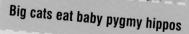
Big cats eat baby pygmy hippos

4 They eat ferns, plants with broad leaves and fallen fruit, whereas common hippos mainly eat grass. Unlike their common hippo cousins, pygmy hippos are good swimmers and also feed on **aquatic** plants.

Small, but very tough!

5 Threats to pygmy hippos include big cats, pythons, crocodiles and, of course, human beings, who are destroying their habitat at a rapid rate.

6 Pygmy hippos living in the wild are now very, very rare. It's thought that there are less than 2,000 of them left. They are classed as **critically endangered**.

7 The good news is that pygmy hippos breed well in captivity and between 1970 and 1991 the population of pygmy hippos born in zoos more than doubled.

PYGMY HIPPOS IN THE WARS

Unfortunately for the pygmy hippo, two of the countries they live in, Liberia and Sierra Leone, have recently had terrible civil wars.

During a civil war, there is no proper government or police force in place to uphold the law, so illegal logging and mining can easily destroy protected habitats, and hungry refugees and soldiers may kill animals like pygmy hippos for food. This is one of the reasons there are so few pygmy hippos left. The good news is that since the wars have ended, life is getting better for both people and pygmy hippos in these countries.

Hanging out with mum

SPOT THE DIFFERENCE

Eyes: On side of head as the pygmy hippo doesn't spend as much time in the water as common hippos do.

Ears and nostrils: The pygmy hippo is able to close these when submerged, like the common hippo.

Body: More pig-like in shape than common hippo. Back slopes more than that of common hippo, possibly to aid movement through dense jungle.

Head: Smaller than common hippo compared to its body, however a pygmy hippo's neck is longer.

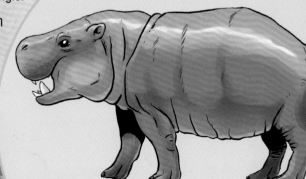

PYGMY HIPPO: FAST FACTS

Where they live: West Africa, in Liberia, Sierra Leone, Côte d'Ivoire and Guinea

Habitat: swamps and tropical rainforests

Length: up to 1.75 metres (5.7 feet)

Weight: up to 275 kilograms (600 pounds)

Life span: up to 35 years in captivity, unknown in the wild

Number of young: average 1

Size at birth: 4.5 to 6.2 kilograms (9.9 to 13.7 pounds)

Status: critically endangered

West Africa

3 THE WATER MOCCASIN

A 'SLIP-ON-SHOE' YOU WOULDN'T WANT TO PUT YOUR FOOT IN

Water moccasins aren't slip-on footwear designed for walking on boggy ground, but are extremely venomous snakes which live in swamps, shallow ponds, ditches and streams.

The scientific Latin name for the water moccasin is *Agkistrodon piscivorus* which means 'hooked-tooth fish eater', but it's also known by lots of other names including cottonmouth, mangrove rattler, trap-jaw, swamp lion, water adder and water viper.

It gets the name 'cottonmouth' from the fact that its mouth, when opened, appears to be lined with soft cotton – but don't be fooled, it isn't!

MEET THE MOCCASIN

Length: Between 76 and 122 centimetres (30 to 48 inches) long.

Eyes: Long, narrow pupils, which take in more light than round pupils, and help the swamp moccasin to see at night when it is most active.

Skin: Black, brown or dark olive-coloured with a light and dark crossed pattern on the back and sides. (This is more visible in the young.)

Belly: Paler than the snake's back and sides, usually the same colour as the ground of its local habitat.

Mouth: White on the inside, used to scare off enemies.

Fangs: Sharp, hollow teeth through which **venom** is injected into prey.

Snout: Pale, with a vertical line by each nostril.

Pits: Heat-sensitive organs on head used to detect prey.

EXTRA SENSORY PERCEPTION

Water moccasins belong to a group of snakes called 'pit vipers', because they have two holes or 'pits' between their eyes and nostrils. These are highly developed heat-sensitive organs which can detect a temperature difference of as little as 0.002° Celcius (0.0036° Farenheit).

These pits work best at night when the prey is warmer than the air that surrounds it, which is when water moccasins do most of their hunting.

Moccasins bite at night!

SNAKE-EAT-SNAKE

Water moccasins mainly eat fish but also gobble up lots of other creatures including rats, squirrels, frogs, rabbits, chipmunks, salamanders, other snakes, birds, turtles, lizards and baby alligators.

The moccasins, in turn, are eaten by bigger animals such as great blue herons, adult alligators, largemouth bass fish and king snakes, (yes, it really is a 'snake-eat-snake' world out there).

To kill its victim, the swamp moccasin holds it in its jaws for as long as it can, to make sure plenty of venom is injected into its flesh. To do this the muscles surrounding its venom sacs contract and squeeze the venom along channels that lead to the base of the fangs. The venom then flows through the hollow fangs, out of a small opening at their tip and into the victim.

Prey animals such as squirrels and rats often fight back, so, to avoid injury once the venom has been injected, the swamp moccasin releases them and lets them then run away. Knowing the prey animal will soon die, the swamp moccasin simply follows its scent until it finds its body. Then, it swallows its victim, head first.

Water moccasins eat chipmunks...

...Blue herons eat water moccasins!

WHAT HAPPENS IF YOU ARE BITTEN BY A WATER MOCCASIN?

There are two sorts of snake venom: **haemotoxic**, which destroys your body tissue and blood cells, and **neurotoxic**, which affects your nervous system. Swamp moccasins have haemotoxic venom, so if you are unlucky enough to be bitten by one you will first suffer bleeding and an excruciating burning pain in the spot where you have been bitten.

Next, the area around your bite will swell to twice its normal size and change to a horrid blue colour. And as if this isn't bad enough, you may also suffer lots of other horrible effects including slurred speech, blurred vision and vomiting.

WHAT TO DO IF YOU ARE BITTEN BY A WATER MOCCASIN

1 Stay calm. If you panic your heart will pump your blood around your body really fast, spreading the venom more quickly.

2 Do not try to suck out the snake venom! You might have seen something like this in a film, but in real life, swallowing snake venom can be as dangerous as being bitten in the first place.

3 Remove all rings and watches. If bitten on a limb, immobilise using an improvised sling. However *do not* apply a **tourniquet** or any excessive pressure.

4 Get to a hospital as quickly as possible. Delay will mean that the venom will begin to spread around your body destroying tissue and blood cells. This could lead to you having the part of your body where you have been bitten removed by **amputation**.

5 At the hospital you will be treated with antibiotics and **antivenin** serum which will stop the effects of the venom.

Go straight to hospital

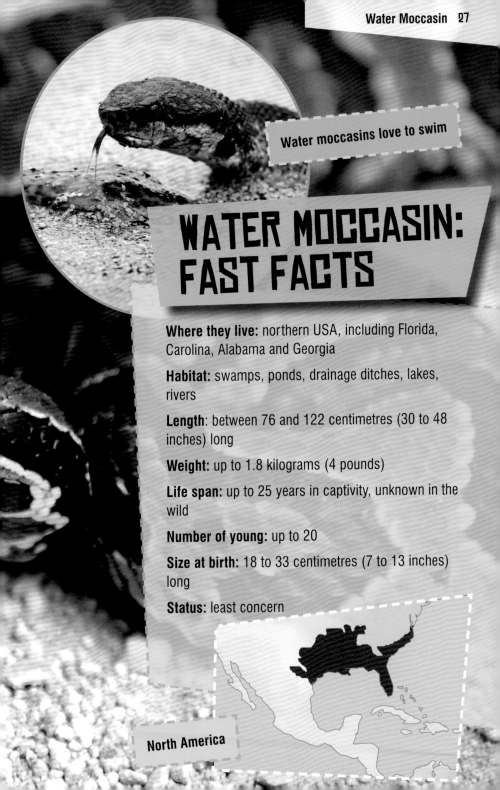

Water moccasins love to swim

WATER MOCCASIN: FAST FACTS

Where they live: northern USA, including Florida, Carolina, Alabama and Georgia

Habitat: swamps, ponds, drainage ditches, lakes, rivers

Length: between 76 and 122 centimetres (30 to 48 inches) long

Weight: up to 1.8 kilograms (4 pounds)

Life span: up to 25 years in captivity, unknown in the wild

Number of young: up to 20

Size at birth: 18 to 33 centimetres (7 to 13 inches) long

Status: least concern

North America

TEN SLITHERY WATER MOCCASIN FACTS

4 Female water moccasins give birth to up to 20 brightly coloured baby snakes which are 18 to 33 centimetres (seven to 13 inches) long.

5 Baby water moccasins waggle their bright yellow, worm-like tails to attract small frogs, fish and animals, then strike at them when they get close enough.

1 Water moccasins aren't aggressive but they will stand their ground if they feel threatened, coiling up and opening their mouths to expose their fangs.

2 If a water moccasin uses up all of its venom during a killing session, it takes about three weeks for its body to replace it.

6 When water moccasins are kept in zoos they are fed frozen rats, mice and hen chicks.

3 Water moccasins are **ovoviviparous**. In other words their eggs develop and hatch inside the mum snake's body and the baby snakes are born live.

8 Water moccasins are excellent swimmers and can bite underwater just as effectively as they can on land. They swim holding their head out of the water at an angle of 45 degrees so they have a good view all around.

Just splashing around

7 During the daytime, water moccasins sunbathe on land to replace body heat lost when they're in the water.

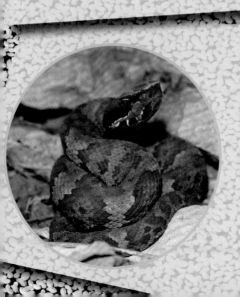

9 When they feel threatened water moccasins spray a pongy liquid called 'musk' from glands near their tails. The liquid is said to smell like billy goats (which are extremely whiffy!).

10 Water moccasins living in colder areas **brumate** during the winter months. One way they make their winter home is to tear bark from rotting pine tree stumps then burrow their way into the soft, pulpy wood.

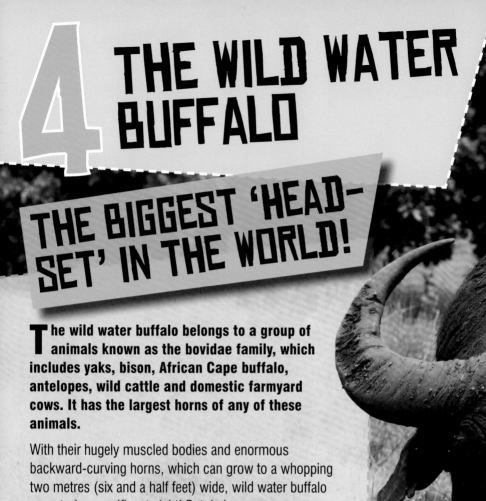

4 THE WILD WATER BUFFALO

THE BIGGEST 'HEAD-SET' IN THE WORLD!

The wild water buffalo belongs to a group of animals known as the bovidae family, which includes yaks, bison, African Cape buffalo, antelopes, wild cattle and domestic farmyard cows. It has the largest horns of any of these animals.

With their hugely muscled bodies and enormous backward-curving horns, which can grow to a whopping two metres (six and a half feet) wide, wild water buffalo are a truly magnificent sight! But, being very, very aggressive indeed, this animal should be treated with great caution.

At one time there were tens of thousands of these fantastic, larger-than-life creatures wandering around tropical and sub-tropical Southeast Asia but there are now only a few thousand left. And all of these surviving wild water buffalo like nothing better than spending their time up to their necks in glorious, gloopy goo!

Squelch!

MUD, MUD, GLORIOUS MUD...

Wild water buffalo have very few sweat glands so they can't rely on **perspiration** to keep them cool, as we humans do. Instead they have to spend much of their time wallowing in the swamps, muddy ponds and marshes of the South Asian tropical and sub-tropical forests.

Water buffalo **graze** at dawn or dusk but during the intense heat of the middle part of the day, quite sensibly, they submerge themselves in the ooze, often with just their nostrils poking out.

Mud evaporates more slowly than water so it's the ideal thing to stay cool in the heat of the tropics (especially when accompanied by a glass of iced lemonade and a tutti-frutti ice cream sundae). It also protects their skin from the swarms of biting insects, which infest their swampy habitats.

HOW TO RECOGNISE A WILD WATER BUFFALO

Weight: A wild water buffalo can weigh from 700 to 1,200 kilograms (1,500 to 2,600 pounds).

Body size: Head-to-body length can be up to three metres (almost ten feet).

Height: Shoulder height can be up to almost two metres (six and a half feet).

Head: Long and narrow with small ears high up on the skull so they don't get full of mud.

Horns: Massive horns which can be up to two metres (six and a half feet) wide. They are used to fend off predators such as tigers and crocodiles. Female wild water buffalo have smaller horns.

Feet: Very large hooved feet **splay** out when walking in mud, to prevent these very heavy animals sinking. Two very flexible joints around the hooves also make it easier to walk in mud, and for the buffalo to run away from predators.

Skin: Ash grey to black. Sparse hair grows forward from the haunches (the tops of the legs).

Tail: 60 to 100 centimetres (23 to 39 inches) long tail with bushy tip to waft away insects.

Oi! What do you think I am?

Asia

WILD WATER BUFFALO: FAST FACTS

Where they live: Southeast Asia, including India, Nepal, Bhutan, Cambodia and Thailand

Habitat: rivers, swamps, marshes and sub-tropical rain forests

Length: 2.4 to 3 metres (7.8 to 10 feet) long, females slightly smaller

Weight: 700 to 1,200 kilograms (1,500 to 2,600 pounds)

Life span: up to 25 years in captivity, average 9 to 12 years in the wild

Number of young: average 1, although sometimes twins

Size at birth: between 30 and 35 kilograms (66 and 77 pounds)

Status: endangered

BUFFALO FAMILIES

Most of the time, adult wild water buffalo live in two separate herds: one for the chaps and one for the mums and their calves. These herds stay fairly close to each other but for most of the year they don't actually mix. The mums' herd consists of about 20 wild water buffalo and is controlled by a bossy older female buffalo known as a 'matriarch' (or 'granny'), who is often accompanied by a single adult and equally scary bull buffalo.

The other younger bull buffalo live in **bachelor** herds of about ten animals and, being typical lads, spend a lot of their time tussling with each other to prove whose 'hardest', but they very rarely injure each other. It's only in the mating season that the real fighting begins.

The mating season takes place between October and November which is the rainy season, ensuring that plenty of vegetation will have grown for the new calves to eat when they're finally born about ten months later. Once the bulls have mated with the females, the the female wild water buffalo drive them off, not wanting to have anything more to do with them. The mums normally give birth to one calf each, which they look after and feed with their milk for six to nine months.

Domestic water buffalo on the move

GOING... GOING... GONE?
HOPEFULLY NOT!

Wild water buffalo are classed as 'endangered' and just a few thousand of them live in protected areas in India, Cambodia, Nepal, Bhutan and a wildlife reserve in Thailand.

The main threats to the survival of wild water buffalo are hunting, loss of habitat and diseases, which they catch from **domestic** water buffalo. They also breed with domestic water buffalo, which results in calves that are no longer truly 'wild'.

The matriarch is in charge

WILD WATER BUFFALO 'LIGHT'

More than 6,000 years ago some very brave farmers in Southeast Asia began catching the big, dangerous wild water buffalo and training them to pull ploughs in their rice fields and provide the power for machines which threshed their rice crops.

As the centuries passed, these 'domesticated' buffalo became smaller, their horns became shorter and their bodies grew more rounded in shape. They also became less aggressive, often being herded by children and becoming friends with their owners. There are even stories of water buffalo saving their owners from attacks by tigers and crocodiles.

The domesticated water buffalo is now known as the 'living tractor of the East' and there are now an astonishing 150 million of them working in Asia.

They're incredibly useful creatures! Their dung is used as a fertilizer and as a fuel when it's dried. Some water buffalo help farmers by pulling carts and carrying goods, whereas other buffalo are used to provide goods such as meat and leather, while their horns are made into things like whistles, bracelets, spoons, combs, buttons and spectacle frames. In India, more people drink domestic water buffalo milk than they do cows' milk.

BRUM... BRUM!

Domestic water buffalo leather is so incredibly thick and strong that it's perfect for making really effective protective helmets, trousers, jackets and gloves for motorcyclists.

YUM... YUM!

Buffalo milk is much richer and creamier than cow's milk and in Italy it's used to make the delicious chewy, stretchy cheese known as mozzarella.

ON YOUR MARKS... GET SET... BUFFALO!

Water buffalo races, known as Kambala, are held every year in the south-western region of Karnataka, India and in Chonburi, Thailand. With as many as 20,000 cheering people watching and betting on the outcome, pairs of domestic water buffalo are yoked together then raced along water-filled tracks by their handlers. However, a lot of people think that this is a cruel and undignified experience for the buffalo.

5 THE MUDSKIPPER

THE FISH THAT WALKS

The idea of a fish that walks on land, jumps in the air, climbs trees and rocks and digs burrows sounds like something from a weird dream or science fiction story. But it's not, because such fish do exist. The totally bizarre little swamp creatures known as mudskippers do all of these things... and more!

Mudskippers are **amphibious** fish. In other words, they live both in water and on land. Many of them live in mangrove swamps or on tidal mudflats where hundreds of them can be seen using their **pectoral** fins to push themselves along, just like a human walking with crutches. In fact, naturalists actually describe this behaviour as 'crutching'.

Mudskippers breathe through gills like other fish do. But they also absorb oxygen through their skin, the linings of their mouths and their throats.

And, like all fish, they must remain wet. So if they're flipping along on land and suddenly find they're getting a bit dry, they simply jump into the nearest pool of water. And, if one of those isn't handy, they just have a good roll around in the mud. Some mudskippers have actually been seen dipping their fins into water then giving the dry areas of their bodies a good wipe with them.

Crutching!

SUPER FISH!

While they're out and about looking for the insects and small **crustaceans** that form their diet, some sorts of mudskippers really do climb up rocks and the roots of mangrove trees. They do this by using their pelvic fins which act like suckers, enabling them to cling to vertical surfaces while at the same time using their fins to pull themselves up.

Mangrove trees have lots of roots

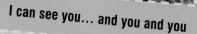

I can see you… and you and you

GOGGLE EYES… AND MORE!

Mudskippers have enormous goggly eyes, which perch on top of their heads. When they're in the water these 'swivel-eyes' act like periscopes, **giving them a 360 degree view of their surroundings whilst the rest of the mudskipper remains hidden under the water.**

When they're on land, in order to keep their eyes moist, these amazing little fish actually roll their eyes under their eyelids so that they can dip them in the water that collects at the bottom of their eye socket. Yes, mudskippers are also the only fish in the whole world that are actually able to blink!

They're also able to move their eyes independently of each other. In other words they can swivel one in one direction and one in the other. How cool is that! And, just as amazingly, the top half of the mudskipper's eye sees in colour while the bottom half only sees in black, white and varying shades of grey. This enables mudskippers to see above and below water at the same time. This really is one seriously weird fish!

MUDSKIPPER: FAST FACTS

Where they live: in tropical to sub-tropical regions from the Atlantic coast of Africa to Australia, Japan and the Pacific islands of Samoa and Tonga

Habitat: hot mangrove forest swamps and mudflats next to the sea

Length: 7 to 25 centimetres (3 to 9 inches) long

Weight: 5 to 12 grams (0.2 to 0.4 ounces)

Life span: estimated to be about 5 to 6 years

Number of young: between 20 and 200 depending on species

Size at birth: when newly hatched 3 to 5 millimetres (0.1 to 0.2 inches) long

Status: least concern

Asia

Africa

STRUTTING THEIR STUFF!

In the mating season male mudskippers become very noticeable, and very active, doing everything they can to attract the attention of all the drop-dead-gorgeous female mudskippers in their neighbourhood.

First, the male mudskippers' colours become brighter, especially the areas around the chin and the throat, which turn a dazzling gold. Then they begin their awesome 'body-popping' routines. They start by performing some low-level wriggling, flipping and press-ups, which they do with the help of their pectoral fins. But they soon move on to using the whole of their muscular little bodies to perform spectacular, massive leaps into the air, some of which are as high as 60 centimetres (24 inches). In no time at all, completely bedazzled by these antics, the female mudskippers become smitten.

Look at meeeeee!

HOME SWEET HOME

Male mudskippers make funnel-shaped nesting burrows in the mud which they use for mating and bringing up their families, as well as staying safe from predators and keeping warm when the weather turns cold. To do this, having no hands, they actually 'dig' the mud by scooping it up into their mouths. They then carry it to the burrow entrance in their mouth where they use it to make a wall, which forms the boundary of a little **reservoir**, ensuring there is still water over the top of the nest at low tides and providing a safe little swimming pool for their growing kids.

A mudskipper burrow

WHEELING ON THE CEILING

At the end of the burrow is a little chamber, where, after the female mudskipper has been lured in by her partner's dazzling disco dancing and mating has taken place, she will lay her eggs. But, in keeping with being one of weirdest creatures on earth, rather than laying them on the floor of the burrow, she lays them on the ceiling. Then, as mudskippers are total rebels in the world of nature, the dad chases her off and takes complete responsibility for bringing up the kids.

BABY MUDSKIPPERS

After a while, tiny mudskipper larvae hatch from the eggs then sort of hang around in their little underground home until they become more like big mudskippers. While this is going on, dad has an important job to do.

Because there is almost no oxygen in the burrow water, he goes up into the big wide world outside, gulps in great mouthfuls of air then brings it back down to the chamber where he releases it, **aerating** the water and ensuring his kids don't suffocate.

When they're not out gulping air or looking for food and pretty lady mudskippers, male mudskippers sit at the entrance to their nest burrows, looking like ferocious guard dogs.

If another mudskipper comes too close, after a bit of angry mouth-gaping and fin waggling, the two mudskippers will begin to fight, seizing hold of each other with their sharp little teeth then hanging on like tiny bull terriers, sometimes for as long as 20 minutes.

GOBSMACKING MUDSKIPPER FACTS

1 The males of one type of mudskipper actually stand on their tails during their 'Oi-look-at-me!' dance sessions to attract a mate, before flopping back onto their sides.

2 Mudskippers can survive high levels of toxic substances such as cyanide, the tiniest bit of which would instantly kill a human.

3 Sometimes mudskippers travel in a line, following a 'leader', so that they end up looking like a crocodile of school children on a day's outing.

4 In Korea and China people make mudskippers into soup and they also eat them in Japan. In order to catch the mudskippers they bury a bamboo pot in the mud so that it looks like a mudskipper burrow then wait for the fish to wiggle their way in. Clever!

Two males getting ready to fight

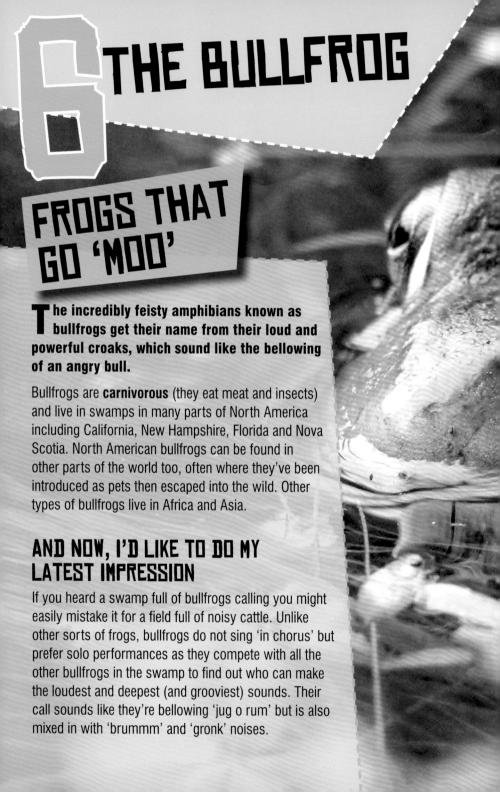

6 THE BULLFROG

FROGS THAT GO 'MOO'

The incredibly feisty amphibians known as bullfrogs get their name from their loud and powerful croaks, which sound like the bellowing of an angry bull.

Bullfrogs are **carnivorous** (they eat meat and insects) and live in swamps in many parts of North America including California, New Hampshire, Florida and Nova Scotia. North American bullfrogs can be found in other parts of the world too, often where they've been introduced as pets then escaped into the wild. Other types of bullfrogs live in Africa and Asia.

AND NOW, I'D LIKE TO DO MY LATEST IMPRESSION

If you heard a swamp full of bullfrogs calling you might easily mistake it for a field full of noisy cattle. Unlike other sorts of frogs, bullfrogs do not sing 'in chorus' but prefer solo performances as they compete with all the other bullfrogs in the swamp to find out who can make the loudest and deepest (and grooviest) sounds. Their call sounds like they're bellowing 'jug o rum' but is also mixed in with 'brummm' and 'gronk' noises.

North America

BULLFROG: FAST FACTS

Where they live: many parts of North America including California, New Hampshire, Florida and Nova Scotia

Habitat: swamps, ponds and lakes

Length: body 9 to 15 centimetres (3.5 to 6 inches) long, legs 18 to 25 centimetres (7 to 10 inches) long

Weight: up to 750 grams (1.6 pounds)

Life span: 8 to 10 years in the wild, up to 16 in captivity

Number of young: each batch of frogspawn can contain up to 25,000 eggs, but relatively few will survive to adulthood

Size at birth: when newly hatched 2 to 3 centimetres (0.88 to 1.1 inches) but tadpoles can grow up to 17.2 centimetres (6.75 inches) long

Status: least concern

FROGS THAT 'SING'

Bullfrogs begin breeding in February and carry on until August. During this time, the male bullfrog is recognisable by its yellow throat while the throat of the female is white.

The males attract females by calling to them with their deep **baritone** voices (but draw the line at singing them soppy love songs). Once they've got together, the male bullfrog climbs onto the female's back and as she lays her eggs in the water he fertilises them. The female bullfrog lays up to 25,000 eggs (just to be on the safe side) that are held together by a sort of jelly, (but not the sort you'd want to eat) and float on the water's surface.

After a few days, the spotty bullfrog tadpoles emerge from the eggs. Compared to other frogs, bullfrog tadpoles take absolutely yonks to turn into froglets, sometimes waiting for as long as three years before they get their legs and other froggy bits. Bullfrog tadpoles become absolutely enormous before they turn into frogs, sometimes growing as long as 17.2 centimetres (6.75 inches)!

A male bullfrog shows off

GREEDY GUTS!

Bullfrogs are incredibly greedy little beasts with huge appetites, eating any other animal they can manage to clobber senseless and stuff into their mouth.

Their victims include mice, shrews, fish, small turtles, snakes, birds, insects, newts, bats and frogs, including other bullfrogs! In order to grab their victims, they leap at them then flip them into their mouths with their long muscular tongues before grasping them with their tiny sharp teeth and biting them to bits (nice!).

Newts, mice and turtles... delicious!

TEN BODACIOUS BULLFROG FACTS

1 If their tails are bitten off by predators, bullfrog tadpoles are able to grow them again (but not straight away).

A huge bullfrog tadpole

2 Bullfrogs are brilliant jumpers, covering distances of up to two metres (16 feet) in a single massive leap (and even more when they're all playing leapfrog).

3 The call of the male bullfrog can be heard from distances of up to a kilometre (over half a mile) away.

4 Bullfrogs have been known to actually leap right out of the water to catch a flying bird or bat.

An Asian banded bullfrog

5 Hungry bullfrogs can clear an entire pond of all its wildlife, eating every other small creature they find from insects to unwary birds.

6 Other types of bullfrogs include African bullfrogs and Asian banded bullfrogs, which are also known as chubby frogs, rice frogs and bubble frogs.

7 Bullfrogs close their nostrils and absorb oxygen through their skin while underwater.

8 African bullfrogs can weigh as much as a whopping two kilograms (4.4 pounds) and reach a humongous 20 centimetres (almost 8 inches) in length.

9 African bullfrogs are even fiercer than the North American sort. One, living at a zoo in South Africa, ate 17 baby cobras.

10 During the dry season, African bullfrogs cover themselves in a cocoon made from their own dead skin, then bury themselves deep in the soil in order to survive.

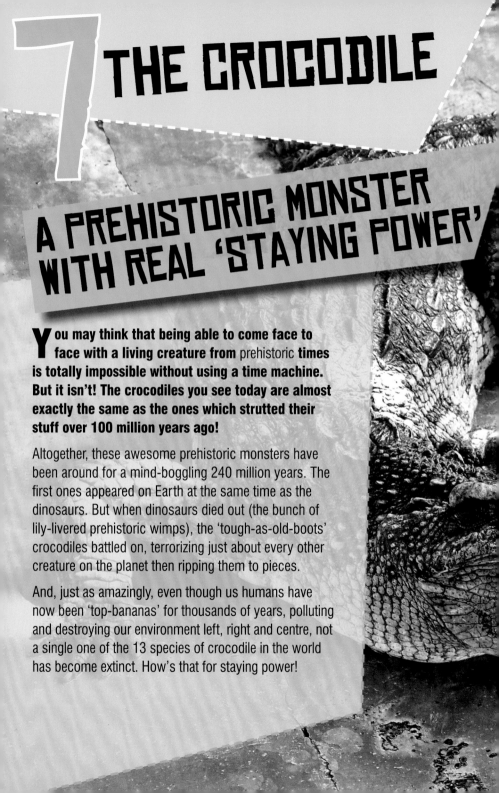

7 THE CROCODILE

A PREHISTORIC MONSTER WITH REAL 'STAYING POWER'

You may think that being able to come face to face with a living creature from prehistoric times is totally impossible without using a time machine. But it isn't! The crocodiles you see today are almost exactly the same as the ones which strutted their stuff over 100 million years ago!

Altogether, these awesome prehistoric monsters have been around for a mind-boggling 240 million years. The first ones appeared on Earth at the same time as the dinosaurs. But when dinosaurs died out (the bunch of lily-livered prehistoric wimps), the 'tough-as-old-boots' crocodiles battled on, terrorizing just about every other creature on the planet then ripping them to pieces.

And, just as amazingly, even though us humans have now been 'top-bananas' for thousands of years, polluting and destroying our environment left, right and centre, not a single one of the 13 species of crocodile in the world has become extinct. How's that for staying power!

I WANNA GO HOME!

Sometimes, when crocodiles and people end up living close to one another, the poor old crocs are moved hundreds of miles away from their original habitats in the hope that they won't come back.

One Australian crocodile became so homesick that it swam 362 kilometres (255 miles) in just 20 days in order to get home. And all without a sat nav!

YOU'RE CROCODILE MEAT, YOU ARE!

Crocodiles have sharp, interlocking teeth which regularly replace themselves if they are damaged or fall out. In its lifetime a crocodile can grow up to 3,000 new gnashers!

THE CUTAWAY CROCODILE

Brain: Small and positioned in the skull so it can heat rapidly when the crocodile is basking in the sun.

Ears: Very sensitive. Have flaps which cover them to stop water going in when the crocodile dives.

Nostrils: Have little plugs which act as valves, closing to stop water going up the croc's nose when it submerges.

Jaw-closing muscles: Anchored beneath the skull. Massive and extremely powerful.

Teeth: Up to 34 on each jaw. Cone-shaped, not all that sharp but very strong, so that crocodile can hang onto prey whilst doing a **death roll**.

Jaw-opening muscles: Small and relatively weak.

Oesophagus (food pipe): Really big so that the croc can swallow prey whole or in huge chunks.

Sensory pits: Bundles of nerve endings in the scales covering the jaw detect vibrations in the water.

Body size: Up to seven metres (23 feet) long.

Weight: Depending on the species, when fully grown can weigh up to 500 kilograms (1,100 pounds).

Trachea (breathing pipe): Pushed off to one side to make room for huge **oesophagus**.

Tail: Almost all muscle with stiff 'propellor' fins made from **keratin**.

Skin: Like a solar panel the skin converts the sun's warmth into 'get up and go' energy by absorbing heat, which is then carried back into the muscles of the croc's body.

Skin: Scales on most of the upper body also contain plates of bone called 'osteoderms', which makes the crocodile's skin incredibly tough. Explorers in days gone by, finding that their old-fashioned guns had no effect on crocodiles, really did believe they were bulletproof.

Stomach: Capable of digesting not only meat, but bone, turtle shell and animal hooves too.

Belly: The underside of a croc is smooth so that it can slide along riverbeds and muddy river banks.

'JAW DROPPING' BITE POWER!

Crocodiles have a stronger bite than any other animal on Earth. When a crocodile crunches down on its victim, it does so with a power of more than 423 kilograms per square centimetre (6,000 pounds per square inch)!

Lots of experiments are carried out to test the bite power of crocodiles and other animals. If you care to get your teeth into them, here are some results:

Crocodile: 423 kg per cm² (6,000 psi)

Grizzly bear: 127 kg per cm² (1,800 psi)

Hyena: 70 kg per cm² (1,000 psi)

Golden eagle: 53 kg per cm²(750 psi)

Great white shark: 42 kg per cm² (600 psi)

Lion: 42 kg per cm² (600 psi)

Human: 12 kg per cm² (170 psi)

kg per cm² = kilograms per square centimetre
psi = pounds per square inch

Crocs can bite *three times* harder than grizzly bears

CROCODILE CURE?

A TV producer filming massive, super-stroppy saltwater crocodiles bashing and biting each other to bits in Australia noticed that, despite their horrendous wounds, they rarely became infected. So she asked a scientist to take some blood samples from the crocodiles to find out why. When the scientist tested the blood she discovered that it contained a substance which killed the sort of bacteria which are resistant to normal **antibiotics**. They've called this crocodillin and hope to use it in drugs to treat human infections.

The Americas

Asia

Africa

CROCODILE: FAST FACTS

Where they live: tropical areas of Africa, Asia, the Americas and Australia

Habitat: rivers, lakes, wetlands and swamps

Length: 1 to 7 metres (3 to 23 feet) long

Weight: up to 500 kilograms (1,100 pounds)

Life span: up to 70 years in the wild, up to 130 in captivity

Number of young: between 25 and 80 eggs, average 50

Size at birth: when newly hatched, can weigh as little as 60 grams (two ounces) and be up to 20 centimetres (7.9 inches) long

Status: least concern to critically endangered (depending on species)

TWELVE SNAPPY CROCODILE FACTS

1 The Ancient Romans used super-strong crocodile skin as armour.

2 Crocodiles can swim at up to ten kilometres (six miles) per hour. Which is pretty fast when you think that top Olympic swimmers only reach about eight kilometres (five miles) per hour.

3 The Ancient Greeks believed that the Nile crocodile would let a little bird called the Egyptian plover hop into its mouth to clean its teeth. Luckily for the plover population, this appears to be untrue.

4 Crocodiles can hold their breath underwater for a couple of hours if they need to.

5 Crocodile's can't stick out their tongues because they're attached to the bottom of their mouths by a thin film-like structure called a membrane.

6 Because crocodiles' jaw-opening muscles are weak it's possible to hold their mouths shut with tape or large rubber bands made from car tyres.

7 Crocodiles can smell food and water from hundreds of metres, and possibly even kilometres away, and can find food hiding in grass using just smell alone.

8 Things which have been found in crocodiles' stomachs include crabs, fish, frogs, insects, pigs, birds, reptiles, turtles, wallabies, other crocodiles, bullets, car number plates and human body parts.

9 Large crocodiles often have stones in their stomachs. It's thought that they are used to help grind up food.

10 Crocodiles sometimes get fur balls in their stomach and regurgitate them, just like a cat does. But unlike cats' fur balls, which are made from their own hair, crocodile fur balls are made up from the fur of their prey animals.

11 Only one per cent of baby crocodiles survive their first year of life. The other 99 per cent are eaten by other animals including fish, lizards, storks and hyenas.

12 Crocodiles have such good hearing that they can hear their babies calling from inside their eggs shells.

8 THE WATER MONITOR

THE LIZARD WHAT IS WELL 'ARD!

If you think crocodiles are scary, wait until you meet this horrendous big swamp beast! Not to be confused with the person a teacher chooses to give out drinks, the water monitor lizard really is a truly terrifying creature.

It's also a truly spectacular creature. It's one of largest lizards in the world, only exceeded in size by the ginormous Komodo dragon. However, although they can grow to an enormous three metres (9.8 feet) long, the average size of water monitors is about one and a half metres (five feet) long.

A mean, lean, eating machine

NO HIDING PLACE!

Water monitor lizards are what are known as 'extreme carnivores'. This means that they will eat any animal they can kill. Their prey includes insects, monkeys, crabs, birds, rats, crocodile eggs, fish, eels, other water monitor lizards, small deer, frogs, snakes, squirrels, young crocodiles and tortoises.

To help them seek out their unlucky victims, these scaly killing-machines have a fluid-filled sensory **Jacobson's organ** in the roof of their mouth and forked tongues, just like snakes. They constantly flick out their tongue picking up smell particles in the air and sending them to the two receptors in their Jacobson's organ. From this they can work out the direction of the scent allowing the water monitor to track its prey, wherever it's hiding.

TWELVE FLABBERGASTING WATER MONITOR FACTS

1 If they come across a recent human grave, water monitor lizards will instantly set about digging it up and eating the body of the person who has been buried in it.

2 Water monitors can swim long distances and are happy in both fresh and saltwater. They sometimes take to the ocean, making their way to remote islands where they set up new colonies.

3 Water monitor lizards will eat the rotting rubbish they find on local garbage dumps. They're also rather partial to gobbling up human poo (so never kiss a water monitor).

4 Water monitors have been seen working as teams when they hunt for crocodile eggs. One water monitor distracts the mum crocodile while the others rush in, dig up the nest and eat the eggs.

5 One 120 centimetre (47 inch) long water monitor lizard killed and ate a snake which was 130 centimetres (51 inches) long.

6 Water monitors swallow their food whole or in large pieces by dislocating their thyroid bone in order to make their throat bigger.

A young water monitor on the beach

7 Water monitors use their tails as weapons and for hanging onto things.

8 When two male water monitors meet, they usually begin fighting ferociously, often tearing great chunks out of each other.

9 Once a water monitor sinks its teeth into you, it is almost impossible to dislodge.

10 Some people turn parts of water monitors into a deadly poison which is used in assassinations.

11 In Sri Lanka, local people protect water monitors because they eat the crabs which would otherwise destroy the banks of their rice fields.

12 One water monitor was seen to hurl itself from a tree branch above a river, actually landing in a passing canoe, much to the alarm of the canoeist.

WHAT HAPPENS WHEN A WATER MONITOR MEETS ITS MATCH?

Despite their ferocity, water monitors do have their enemies, including crocodiles and large birds of prey. Young water monitors are also a favourite snack for herons.

When a water monitor is attacked, it first inflates its throat and hisses loudly whilst lashing out with its tail. If it can, it then makes its escape by dashing up a tree and leaping from branch to branch, then dropping into the water. However, if cornered it will fight to the death, biting and clawing at its attacker. If it's caught by its tail, it simply lets its attacker pull it off, then scuttles away tailless, as other lizards do.

Lizards use their tongues to smell

Water monitors love termites

THEY JUST KEEP COMING!

Water monitors breed from April to October. Large females can lay their own weight in eggs, up to 40 at a time! And as you'd expect with water monitors, mating involves lots of vicious scratching and biting.

When they're looking for somewhere to nest, the females carry their tails high above their heads. They build nests in rotting logs, tree stumps and termite mounds or dig nine metre (29 feet) long burrows in riverbanks. Then, after about five weeks, they lay their eggs. When they've hatched, the young water monitors, which are more brightly coloured than the adults, climb trees to keep out of harm's way.

WATER MONITOR CONSERVATION

In Asia, some poor rural people hunt water monitors for food as their meat is a good source of protein. Their skins are also used for leather goods, religious ceremonies, medicine and potions.

More than one million skins are traded every year, mostly in Indonesia. However, the tough, thick skins of larger monitors aren't at all easy to turn into leather goods which means the large females, which lay the most eggs, manage to survive and carry on churning out new water monitors.

A QUICK FINAL WORD ABOUT THIS 'COLD-BLOODED' KILLER

Like all the reptiles mentioned in this book, water monitors are **cold-blooded**. But this doesn't mean that their blood is actually cold.

Their temperature changes according to their surroundings. Water monitors make sure they remain in **micro-climates**, which keep them warm enough to suit their very active lifestyles.

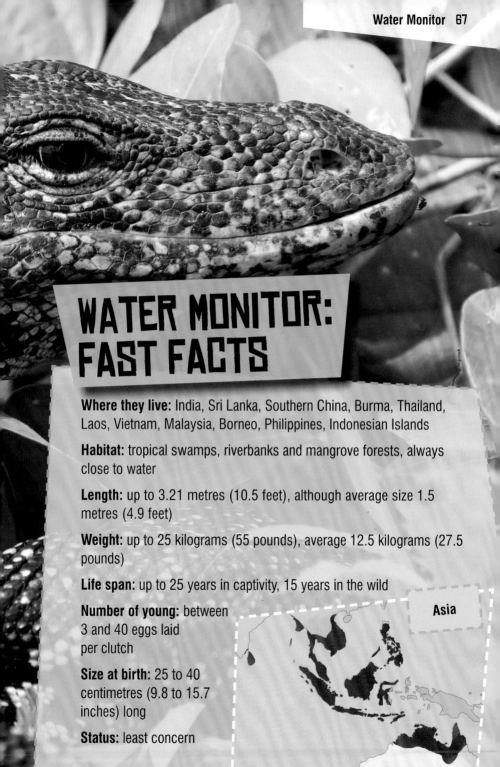

WATER MONITOR: FAST FACTS

Where they live: India, Sri Lanka, Southern China, Burma, Thailand, Laos, Vietnam, Malaysia, Borneo, Philippines, Indonesian Islands

Habitat: tropical swamps, riverbanks and mangrove forests, always close to water

Length: up to 3.21 metres (10.5 feet), although average size 1.5 metres (4.9 feet)

Weight: up to 25 kilograms (55 pounds), average 12.5 kilograms (27.5 pounds)

Life span: up to 25 years in captivity, 15 years in the wild

Number of young: between 3 and 40 eggs laid per clutch

Size at birth: 25 to 40 centimetres (9.8 to 15.7 inches) long

Status: least concern

Asia

9 THE 'EXTRAORDINARY' SHOEBILL

THAT BEAK... IS WELL BIG!

A naturalist writing about shoebills in a paper for a zoo in 1851 described it as 'the most extraordinary bird I have seen for many years', which is no doubt what most people think when they set eyes on this bizarre creature for the first time.

With their giant, shoe-shaped beaks, the massive African wading birds known as shoebills are truly prehistoric looking. Between 5,000 and 8,000 of them live in **impenetrable** swamps in places like Congo, Sudan and Zambia where they hunt for prey which includes frogs, other water birds, rats and lungfish, one of their favourite snacks.

To catch their victims, shoebills stand motionless in the mud or on banks of floating vegetation looking for signs of movement. The moment they spot a victim they pounce with incredible speed, grasping it in their huge, powerful **mandibles** then piercing and crushing it with their razor-sharp bill edges and 'bill tooth', a sharp, nail-like hook at the end of their bill.

Look at the size of that bill!

BREEDING

Shoebills tend to spend their time on their own and only get together to mate. They build their nests out of grass on higher, dry areas or floating platforms of weeds. The mum shoebill lays about three eggs, which both parents **incubate** for about a month.

Baby shoebills are helpless for some time after hatching and only learn to fly when they are about three months old. When they're calling for food they make a 'hiccuping' noise (and are then lovingly 'burped' by their parents).

FIVE SCINTILLATING SHOEBILL FACTS

1 Shoebills are generally fairly quiet birds but do occasionally make whining or 'mooing' sounds.

4 When they build their 1.5 metre (4.9 feet) **diameter** nests, shoebills work plant stems into it by jumping on them to flatten them, then poking them into the nest with their feet.

2 When they're mating, shoebills carry out a display known as 'bill clattering'. This involves them throwing their heads straight back making a clattering 'dok-dok-dok' noise which sounds like a machine gun being fired.

3 Shoebills like to hunt for prey in water which is low in oxygen, as this means that fish have to surface to take in air quite regularly, making themselves easier to catch.

5 When it's really hot, parent shoebills drink water then regurgitate it onto their eggs to keep them cool.

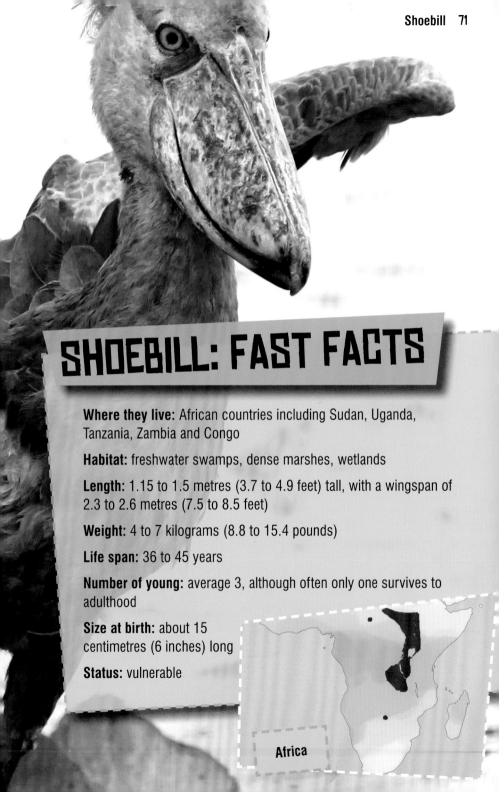

SHOEBILL: FAST FACTS

Where they live: African countries including Sudan, Uganda, Tanzania, Zambia and Congo

Habitat: freshwater swamps, dense marshes, wetlands

Length: 1.15 to 1.5 metres (3.7 to 4.9 feet) tall, with a wingspan of 2.3 to 2.6 metres (7.5 to 8.5 feet)

Weight: 4 to 7 kilograms (8.8 to 15.4 pounds)

Life span: 36 to 45 years

Number of young: average 3, although often only one survives to adulthood

Size at birth: about 15 centimetres (6 inches) long

Status: vulnerable

Africa

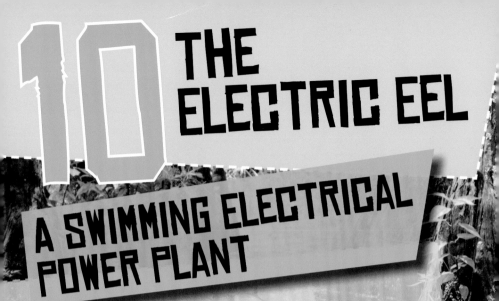

10 THE ELECTRIC EEL

A SWIMMING ELECTRICAL POWER PLANT

Electric eels live in the swamps of South America and can grow to a whopping two and a half metres (over eight feet) long.

What's most remarkable about these huge and terrifying creatures is the fact that they're able to generate more electricity than any other animal on Earth, enough to kill an adult crocodile! As well as using this power to stun or kill the animals it eats, the electric eel uses it to defend itself against enemies (and to charge its iPhone).

SOME 'SHOCKING' REVELATIONS ABOUT ELECTRIC EELS

Electric eels look like eels and are called eels but they're not an eel at all. They are actually a fish which is related to the catfish and knifefish.

The name for a group of electric eels is a swarm, just like wasps and bees (although more fishy).

Unlike most other species, male electric eels are much smaller than the ladies, and do most of the looking after of the kids.

Tough enough to kill a crocodile

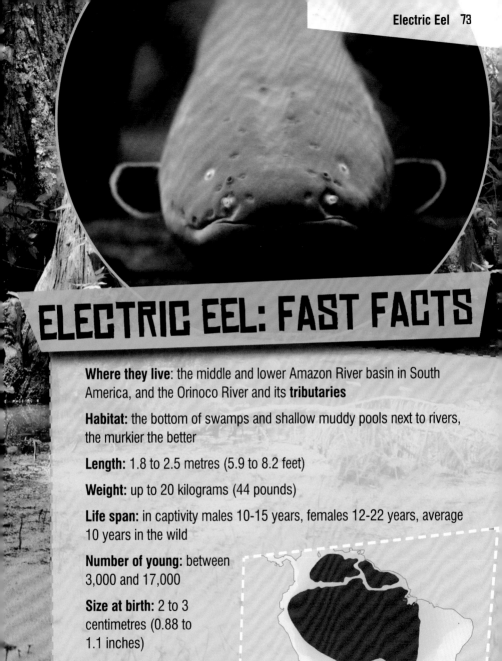

ELECTRIC EEL: FAST FACTS

Where they live: the middle and lower Amazon River basin in South America, and the Orinoco River and its **tributaries**

Habitat: the bottom of swamps and shallow muddy pools next to rivers, the murkier the better

Length: 1.8 to 2.5 metres (5.9 to 8.2 feet)

Weight: up to 20 kilograms (44 pounds)

Life span: in captivity males 10-15 years, females 12-22 years, average 10 years in the wild

Number of young: between 3,000 and 17,000

Size at birth: 2 to 3 centimetres (0.88 to 1.1 inches)

Status: least concern

South America

Electric eels aren't actually eels

Their tiny eyes can't see well

EELECTRICITY

The electric eel has about 6,000 disc-shaped muscle cells called electrocytes, packed into three pairs of specialised electric organs situated in its abdomen.

Each cell acts like a tiny battery and is able to produce 0.1 volts of electricity. So it's possible for an electric eel to generate up to about 650 volts of electrical power. That's *three times* as much electricity as would flow out of a wall socket when an electrical appliance such as a vacuum cleaner or TV is plugged in.

So if you were to enter a swamp where an electric eel was zapping out shocks it would probably result in certain death. The electricity flows out of the eel for a very brief two milliseconds, but it's able to zap out about 150 shocks in an hour.

LITTLE 'SPITTING' IMAGES

When they're ready to start a family, male electric eels make nests out of their own spit! Then the female lays her eggs in the **saliva** nest and the male hangs about to make sure no other creatures (including older electric eel hatchlings) eat them.

After a while about 3,000 baby eels hatch from the eggs, (imagine the mammoth task of giving them all names). Now, either mum or dad guards the nest until their little wigglers are about 15 centimetres (5.9 inches) long.

ELECTRIC EELS IN CAPTIVITY

To protect them from getting electrocuted by the eels they care for, zoo workers wear rubber gloves and use feeding tongs, nets and tank cleaners that are made from materials that do not conduct electricity.

They also 'target train' the eels using a plastic bottle with rocks inside which the eel has been trained to associate with food. On hearing the vibrations of the rocks in the bottle, the eel swims towards it, then remains very still until it is rewarded with a fish.

AN ELECTRIC EEL: THE WORKS

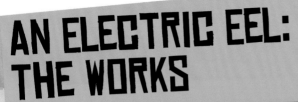

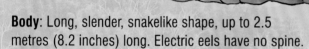

Body: Long, slender, snakelike shape, up to 2.5 metres (8.2 inches) long. Electric eels have no spine.

Front: The front 20 per cent of the body contains the eel's brain, heart, and digestive system.

Back: The back 80 per cent contains three pairs of organs made up of muscles called electrocytes which produce an electric current.

Skin: Greyish brown on top and yellow or orange on the belly.

Head: Flattened with a bright orange throat and a square mouth right at the end of the snout.

Teeth: Electric eels have no teeth, so they have to suck in their prey and swallow it whole. Gulp!

Eyes: Bright green and relatively small. Electric eels have very bad eyesight.

SEVEN SIZZLING ELECTRIC EEL FACTS

1 Electric eels can produce enough electricity to kill a horse, stun a fish 20 metres (65.6 feet) away or give a human being a heart attack.

2 A public aquarium in Japan linked their eel tank to their Christmas tree and powered its lights with electricity from the electric eels.

3 Electric eels have very poor eyesight but they make up for this by using electricity to navigate (and wearing really big spectacles).

4 Because they produce so much electricity, eels function just like the battery you'd put in a TV controller, their head being the positive pole and their tail the negative pole.

An electric eel can kill a horse

5 The fish gills of electric eels are so small that they don't work at all well, so they have to rise to the surface every few minutes or so to gulp air into their mouths, after which they sink back to the bottom. If they don't do this, they'll drown in about ten minutes.

6 Dead electric eels remain 'live' for some time and can still give you a mighty electrical shock.

7 No one's quite sure why electric eels are able to electrocute other animals without actually electrocuting themselves.

11

THE ALLIGATOR SNAPPING TURTLE

A VERY SNAPPY LITTLE 'DINOSAUR'

Alligator snapping turtles are the largest freshwater turtles in the world and can sometimes be as long as 80 centimetres (31.5 inches).

With their thick scaly tails, massive heads, long, thick, spiked shells and beak-like jaws, these incredibly primitive-looking reptiles really do resemble small dinosaurs.

FANCY A GAME OF SNAP! OR MAYBE... FISH?

Attached to the tip of an alligator snapping turtle's tongue is a bright pink piece of flesh which looks exactly like a worm. The rest of the turtle, including the inside of its mouth, is so well camouflaged that it looks like a stone as it lies at the bottom of the swamp.

To attract prey, the alligator snapping turtle simply remains motionless with its mouth open and its pretend worm wiggling furiously as it waits for a curious fish to be attracted by this tasty looking morsel. All the passing fish can see is the worm, so it goes to investigate. Then, when the unsuspecting fish is close enough, the turtle's mouth snaps shut with astonishing speed and power! The fish is then swallowed whole, sliced in two or spiked on the sharp tips of the turtle's 'beak'. Alligator snapping turtles also eat frogs, worms, mussels and other turtles.

North America

Its worm-like tongue lures prey

ALLIGATOR SNAPPING TURTLE: FAST FACTS

Where they live: the southern states of the USA

Habitat: swamps, canals, lakes and rivers

Length: 66 to 80 centimetres (26 to 31.5 inches)

Weight: 80 to 100 kilograms
(176 to 220 pounds)

Life span: 20 to 70 years (possibly more)

Number of young: between 10 and 80

Size at birth: 5 centimetres (2 inches)

Status: vulnerable

THE PATTER OF TINY TURTLE FEET

Like many animals, alligator snapping turtles mate when the weather warms up in the spring. After mating, the male wanders off never to return!

About two months later the female alligator snapping turtle leaves the water and digs a hole in which she lays her eggs. Having covered the eggs with sand, leaves and mud she returns to the swamp (leaving her kids to sort out their own lives).

About 100 days later, the baby turtles break out of their egg shells, then scamper back to the water as fast as their little legs will carry them. The babies take about 12 years to grow up and start families of their own.

During this time, the unluckier ones get eaten by snakes, birds and mammals such as otters and rats. However, the only enemy the adult alligator snapping turtle has is the humans who hunt them for their shells and meat.

Some turtles could be up to 150 years old

FIVE SNAPPY FACTS

1 Snapping alligator turtle eggs which develop at high temperatures tend to result in female baby turtles, while those which develop at low temperatures tend to result in male baby turtles.

2 Alligator snapping turtles were once referred to as 'Ograbmes' by the early settlers in North America. (Say it out loud if you don't get it!)

3 Alligator snapping turtles remain motionless for so long that the green plant known as algae grows on their shells.

4 It's reported that some alligator snapping turtles have been found with bullets from the American Civil War lodged in their shells. If true, this would mean that they are able to live for up to 150 years.

5 Alligator snapping turtles can't pull their heads into their shells like other turtles can.

12

THE GREEN ANACONDA

CALL ME 'CRUSHER'!

The South American green anaconda belongs to the boa constrictor family of snakes which all share the habit of crushing their prey to death.

The green anaconda is possibly the longest snake in the world, reportedly reaching lengths of almost nine metres (29.5 feet) or more. It's also the fattest snake in the world. The reticulated python is the only snake which grows to about the same length as the green anaconda, but the anaconda is almost twice as heavy.

EASY SQUEEZY

Anacondas eat wild pigs, deer, birds, turtles, capybara (large rodents) and caimans (a type of crocodile). Some people have even reported them crushing and eating the ferocious big cats known as jaguars.

Once the anaconda spots its intended victim, it grabs it in its jaws and begins to wrap its enormous muscular body around and around its prey.

Eventually the animal is squeezed so hard that it's completely unable to breathe and dies of suffocation. Next the anaconda opens its jaws to an incredibly wide 180 degree angle so that it's able to swallow its victim whole. Once the animal is swallowed, it's often possible to make out its shape inside the bulging anaconda.

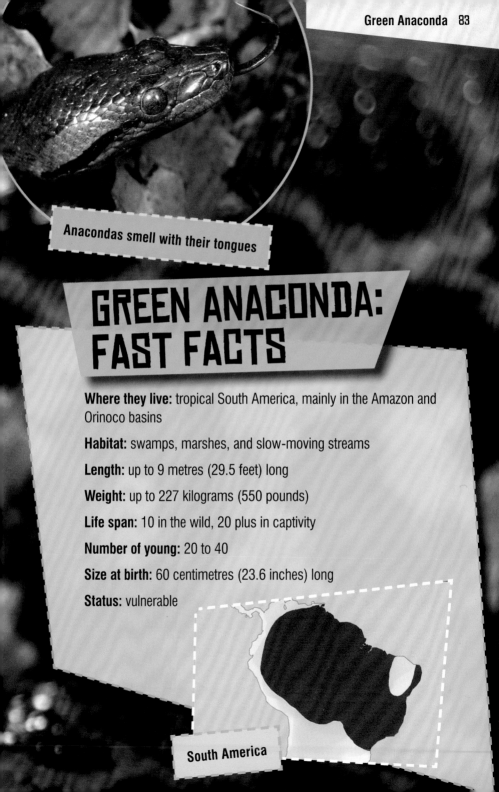

Anacondas smell with their tongues

GREEN ANACONDA: FAST FACTS

Where they live: tropical South America, mainly in the Amazon and Orinoco basins

Habitat: swamps, marshes, and slow-moving streams

Length: up to 9 metres (29.5 feet) long

Weight: up to 227 kilograms (550 pounds)

Life span: 10 in the wild, 20 plus in captivity

Number of young: 20 to 40

Size at birth: 60 centimetres (23.6 inches) long

Status: vulnerable

South America

SIX AWESOME ANACONDA FACTS

1 The reason anacondas can open their mouths so incredibly wide is that their upper and lower jaws are attached by really stretchy **ligaments** which are like very strong elastic.

2 Anacondas can quickly regurgitate an animal they've swallowed if they're disturbed or frightened.

3 Anacondas have about 100 backward-curving teeth, which ensure they can get a get a really firm grip on their prey.

5 Female anacondas occasionally eat male anacondas when they've just finished mating.

Needle sharp teeth

6 Anacondas can hold their breath for 15 minutes. Because of this, sometimes rather than suffocating their victims, they drown them instead.

4 From birth to adulthood, an anaconda grows 500 times bigger. That's like a human baby ending up weighing a whopping 1,750 kg (3,858 pounds) when it's grown up.

TYING THE 'KNOT'

Green anacondas spend most of their time on their own. But, between April and May, male anacondas go looking for females to mate with. Once she's mated, a female anaconda produces between 20 and 40 eggs inside her body. The eggs take between eight and 12 weeks to develop then hatch while they are still inside the mother's body. She then gives birth to tiny snakes, each one about 60 centimetres (23.6 inches) long.

Sometimes lots of male anacondas are so desperate to mate with the same female anaconda that they all end up wrapping themselves around her at the same time. The resulting tangle of snakes is known as a 'breeding ball' or a 'knot'. These knots look rather like slow motion wrestling matches and sometimes the anacondas can remain tangled up in them for a whole month.

13

THE SURINAM TOAD

FLAT-PACK TOADS

No doubt there are creatures living on planets in faraway galaxies which are even weirder than Surinam toads.

However, few creatures on planet Earth can match these bizarre and awesome amphibians for their strange appearance... and their even stranger breeding behaviour.

Surinam toads really do look like they've had an unfortunate encounter with the tyres of a large motor vehicle from which they've never really recovered. To put it another way, they're very, very flat.

They spend most of their lives lying on the bottom of swamps, pretending to be a dead leaf (or possibly a dead toad), only rising to the surface every 30 minutes or so to take in air.

One of the only other times they do appear to show any sign of life is when a tasty fish, worm or small crustacean happens to swim past, in which case they lunge at it, scooping it into their mouths with their long fingers.

Is it a leaf, or a toad?

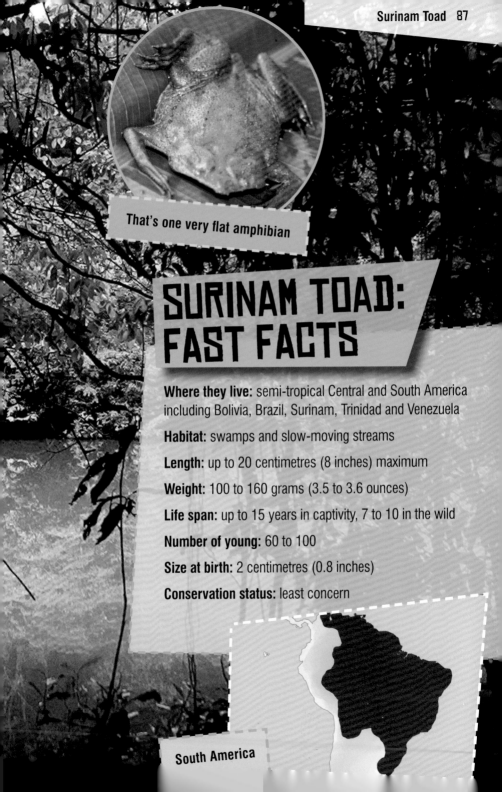

That's one very flat amphibian

SURINAM TOAD: FAST FACTS

Where they live: semi-tropical Central and South America including Bolivia, Brazil, Surinam, Trinidad and Venezuela

Habitat: swamps and slow-moving streams

Length: up to 20 centimetres (8 inches) maximum

Weight: 100 to 160 grams (3.5 to 3.6 ounces)

Life span: up to 15 years in captivity, 7 to 10 in the wild

Number of young: 60 to 100

Size at birth: 2 centimetres (0.8 inches)

Conservation status: least concern

South America

A BACK FULL OF BABY TOADS

In order to attract mates, male Surinam toads don't croak like most frogs do. Instead they make a sharp clicking sound by 'snapping' a little bone in their throat which (along with their stunning good looks) female Surinam toads find utterly irresistible.

In no time at all, male and female toads are pairing off at the bottom of the swamp. Next, they rise to the surface, nonchalantly performing graceful somersaults as they do. And this is where things really do get weird. During each somersault, the female lays between three and seven eggs.

But, rather than sticking them to bits of vegetation, as most frogs do, she lays them directly onto the belly of the male toad. Then he fertilises them, but he's not finished yet.

Now it's time for the really tricky part. Taking enormous care not to drop them, the male carefully rolls the eggs from his own belly onto the female's back. And rather than just rolling off, they instantly become firmly attached to her spongy skin. This little ritual is repeated until mum's popped out a total of between 60 and 100 eggs, which the male has duly fertilised and stuck to her back. Then, his job done, the male tootles off, never to be seen again.

Check out those toad nodes

Eggs turning into tiny toads

TOTALLY WEIRD TOAD NODES

Now, if it's possible, things get even stranger. Twenty-four hours after mating, rather like a scene from *Alien Toads from Planet Weird*, the skin on mum toad's back begins to change shape as it swells and grows over each egg. Soon, a cosy little pocket, or personal toad 'node', has formed over each egg, so it can develop, safe from hungry fish and other predators. Now, with her eggs securely stashed in the honeycomb of pockets which cover her back, mum gets back to the busy, ultra-stressful daily routine of a Surinam toad, i.e. hanging around at the bottom of the swamp hoping something tasty will swim past.

TADPOLE FREE ZONE

While mum is busy hanging out at the bottom of the swamp, the eggs begin to develop in their individual little pockets.

But instead of going through all that tedious tadpole malarkey, like ordinary frogs do, Surinam toads-in-the-making skip this bit completely and, a few months later, each pocket contains a living baby toad. Soon mum toad's back is rippling all over as the excited little toads begin moving around inside their little toad 'nodes', all desperate to get out into the big wide world so that they can get on with the important business of pretending to be dead leaves.

THE TOAD EXPLODES [WELL, SORT OF...]

Finally, the great day arrives. About five months after mum and dad did all that somersaulting, two centimetre (0.8 inch) long baby toads begin breaking out of their toad-nodes and swimming off to their new solitary existences, ungratefully leaving mum with a back full of grotty great holes, which even a male Surinam toad might find a bit off-putting.

But she has nothing to worry about. Soon she will shed her battlefield of a back and its cruddy craters, growing fresh skin to replace it and become as desirable and attractive as she ever was (well, at least to other Surinam toads).

As Charles Darwin might have said (although he probably didn't), 'That is well weird!'

Charles Darwin

Baby toads leave their nodes

SQUELCH

We've only mentioned a few of the amazing animals which can be found lurking in the swamps of planet Earth. There hasn't been room to talk about the ferocious African lungfish, the favourite snack of the shoebill. In addition to gills, these fearsome creatures also have a couple of lungs,which enable them to survive if the water happens to dry up! Then there are the swamp-dwelling mass killers known as mosquitoes, which have killed millions of people and are the most dangerous animal on Earth. And lots more awesome and scary creatures. Yes, swamps can be very dangerous places. But they're certainly never, ever boring!

ABOUT ZSL

The Zoological Society of London (ZSL) is a charity that provides conservation support for animals both in the UK and worldwide. We also run ZSL London Zoo and ZSL Whipsnade Zoo.

By buying this book, you have helped us to raise money to continue our conservation work with animals around the world.

Find out more at **zsl.org**

ZSL
LIVING CONSERVATION

ZSL
**LONDON
ZOO**

ZSL
**WHIPSNADE
ZOO**

FURTHER INFORMATION:

ZSL London Zoo
Outer Circle, Regent's Park,
London, NW1 4RY, UK
www.zsl.org/london

ZSL Whipsnade Zoo
Dunstable, Bedfordshire,
LU6 2LF, UK
www.zsl.org/whipsnade

www.storiesfromthezoo.com

GLOSSARY

abdomen – also called the 'belly', the area between the chest and hips

aerate – circulate air

amphibian – cold-blooded creature that lives in or near water

amputation – surgical removal of a limb

antibiotic – medicine that destroys bacteria and disease

antivenin – a substance that stops the effects of a **venom**

aquatic – connected with, or dependent on water

bachelor – a male animal without a mate

baritone – a low or deep voice

brumate (brumation) – when a reptile slows down its **metabolism** during cold weather so it does not need to eat

calf – young cow, buffalo, elephant, whale, hippo or giraffe

canine teeth – pointed teeth used for tearing meat

carnivorous – feeding on the flesh of animals and/or **invertebrates**

cold-blooded – used to describe animals with a body temperature that is dependent on the surrounding temperature

critically endangered – used to describe species that are at high risk of extinction

crustacean – an animal with an **exoskeleton** instead of a spine that lives in or near water

death roll – when a crocodile or alligator spins over and over with its prey clamped in its jaws

diameter – the width or thickness of something

DNA – the genetic instructions that make up all **organisms**

domestic (animals) – kept as a farm animal or a pet

electrocyte – modified nerve or muscle cells that can create an electric current

evolutionary route – the path a species takes as it changes and adapts over time

exoskeleton – a hard covering that provides support and protection

extinct (extinction) – when a species has completely died out

fertilise – when eggs and sperm unite to allow a new individual to start developing

graze – to feed on grass and other green plants

haemotoxic – a substance that causes blood poisoning

herbivore – an animal that feeds mostly or only on grass and plants

impenetrable – something that can't be entered or changed

incubate – to keep eggs (or premature organisms) at a stable temperature until they are able to survive unaided

invertebrate – a creature without a spine, such as insects, worms, crabs octopuses and snails

Jacobson's organ – a fluid-filled sac in the roof of the mouth of many animals, especially reptiles, used for smelling

juvenile – young or youthful

keratin – a **protein** found in hair, nails and claws

larva (plural: larvae) – the juvenile stage of an insect or amphibian

larynx – voice box

ligament – a stretchy band of muscle that holds bones and organs in place

mandibles – jaws

mangrove swamp – boggy area where mangrove trees grow

marrow – fatty tissue that fills the inside of bones

mate – breed or reproduce

matriarch – female head of the family, usually the oldest

metabolism – the uptake of food and disposal of waste products

micro-climate – a climate specific to a particular region

minted – to cast (produce) coins

multi-chambered – divided into many sections

naturalist – a person who studies nature

neurotoxic – a substance that causes nerve damage

oesophagus – food pipe

organism – a living thing

ovoviviparous – when young develop inside eggs that are kept inside the mother's body until they are ready to hatch

oxygen – a gas that is found in the air we breathe

pectoral (fin) – a pair of fins located directly below or behind the gills

pelvic – relating to the pelvis (hips)

periscope – equipment used to view above eye-level using mirrors, prisms and lenses (as found on submarines)

perspiration – sweat

plough – the name of the tool used to prepare land for sowing seeds

predator – an animal that hunts, kills and eats other animals for food

prehistoric – relating to the time before history was written down

prey – an animal or invertebrate hunted for food

protein – a complex natural substance that makes up DNA among other things

reservoir – area where fluid is stored

saliva – spit

sinuous – winding and curvy

species – a kind, sort or variety of something

splay – to spread out

territory – an area of land occupied by a particular individual or group

thresh – to separate the grain or seeds from the straw and husks of a cereal plant

tourniquet – device for stopping the flow of blood

trachea – wind (breathing) pipe

tributary – a stream that flows into a bigger river

vegetation – plants

venom – a poisonous fluid produced by an animal or insect that is injected into prey or an attacker

vulnerable species – a species that is likely to become endangered

SPECIAL THANKS

To Ian Stephen, Curator of Herpetology at ZSL London Zoo.